Distance Learning

by Julie Murray

Abdo Kids Jumbo is an Imprint of Abdo Kids
abdobooks.com

abdobooks.com

Published by Abdo Kids, a division of ABDO, P.O. Box 398166, Minneapolis, Minnesota 55439.
Copyright © 2021 by Abdo Consulting Group, Inc. International copyrights reserved in all countries.
No part of this book may be reproduced in any form without written permission from the publisher.
Abdo Kids Jumbo™ is a trademark and logo of Abdo Kids.

Printed in the United States of America, North Mankato, Minnesota.

052020

092020

 THIS BOOK CONTAINS
RECYCLED MATERIALS

Photo Credits: Getty Images, iStock, Shutterstock

Production Contributors: Teddy Borth, Jennie Forsberg, Grace Hansen
Design Contributors: Dorothy Toth, Pakou Moua

Library of Congress Control Number: 2020936701
Publisher's Cataloging-in-Publication Data

Names: Murray, Julie, author.

Title: Distance learning / by Julie Murray

Description: Minneapolis, Minnesota : Abdo Kids, 2021 | Series: The Coronavirus | Includes online
resources and index.

Identifiers: ISBN 9781098205515 (lib. bdg.) | ISBN 9781098205652 (ebook) | ISBN 9781098205720
(Read-to-Me ebook)

Subjects: LCSH: Distance education--Juvenile literature. | Social distance--Juvenile literature. |
Videoconferencing--Juvenile literature. | Coronavirus infections--Juvenile literature. | Communicable
diseases--Prevention--Juvenile literature. | Epidemics--Juvenile literature.

Classification: DDC 371.35--dc23

Table of Contents

Distance Learning

Distance learning is a **remote** way of learning. It allows students to learn without being in a classroom. It uses technology to connect students with teachers and classmates.

Distance learning was widely used during the **COVID-19** pandemic. Many states closed schools. Students and teachers stayed home. Students learned online.

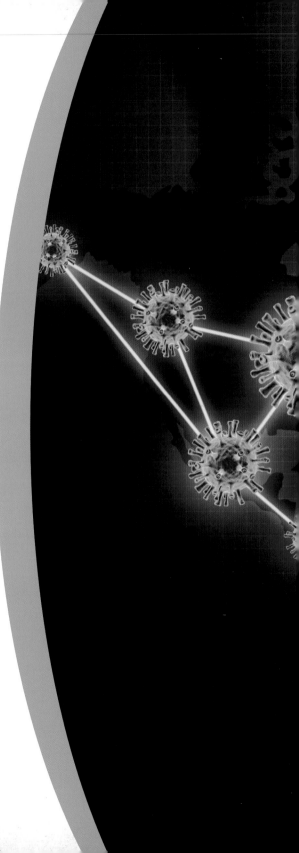

What Is a Pandemic?

A pandemic is a global outbreak of a disease. This can happen when a **virus** infects people and quickly spreads.

8

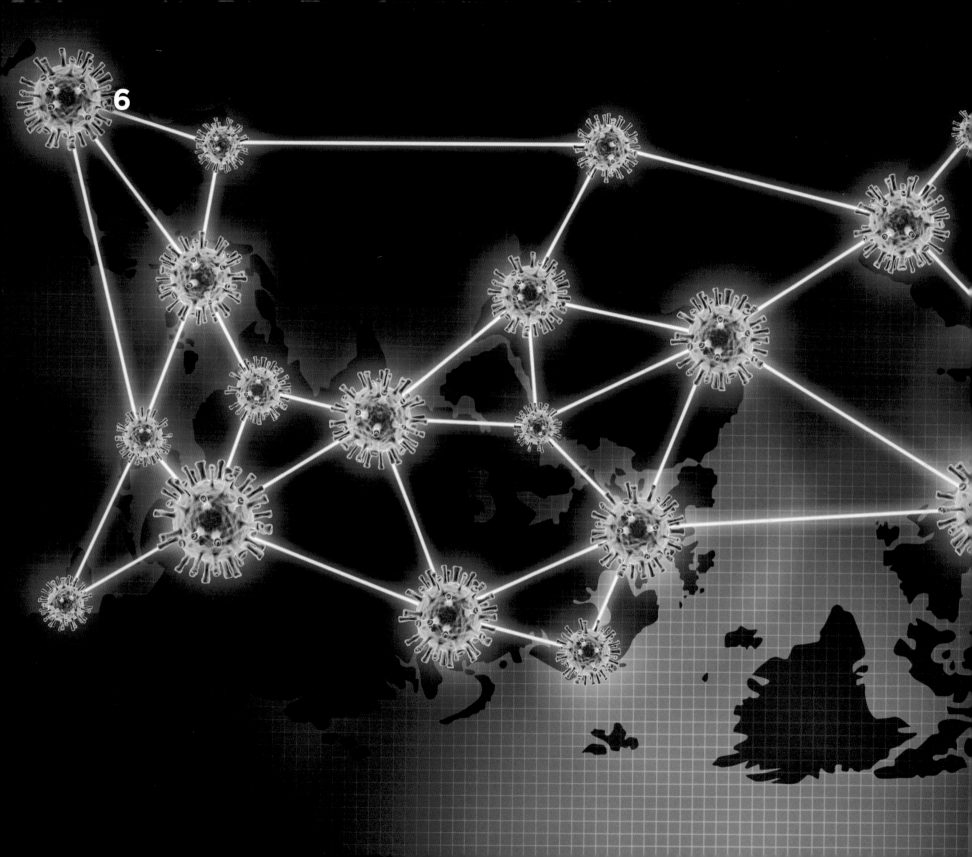

The **COVID-19** illness is caused by a new **virus**. It became a pandemic on March 11, 2020. Many places closed, including schools.

Ways to Learn

When schools are closed, teachers can use video chats that include the entire class. Students can see one another and join in group discussions.

13

Students go online to get their assignments. They can also watch a teacher's pre-recorded video. They email a photo or video of their completed work.

Students communicate with teachers and classmates through different **apps**. They are able to stay connected even though they are apart.

17

Positive Outcomes

In distance learning, students work by themselves much of the time. They learn new skills, like how to be more **responsible** and organized.

19

Distance learning allows students to connect with one another in different ways. They discover new ways of learning too!

Let's Review!

- Distance learning is a **remote** way to attend school. Students use technology to connect with teachers and classmates.

- A pandemic is a disease that spreads to many people around the world.

- **COVID-19** became a pandemic in 2020. Many schools used distance learning during this time.

- Teachers can use video chats and **apps** to connect with students while distance learning.

- Students use the internet, email, and other apps. They are able to complete assignments this way. They can also work with their classmates.

22

Glossary

app – short for application, a program that performs a certain task.

COVID-19 – short for Coronavirus Disease 2019, the illness caused by a new strain of coronavirus. Common symptoms include fever, cough, and shortness of breath. More serious symptoms can occur in some people.

remote – at a far distance.

responsible – able to take care of certain things on one's own.

virus – a tiny organism that can reproduce only in living cells. Viruses can cause illnesses in humans, animals, and plants.

Index

Abdo Kids
ONLINE
FREE! ONLINE MULTIMEDIA RESOURCES

Visit **abdokids.com** to access crafts, games, videos, and more!

Use Abdo Kids code

TDK5522

or scan this QR code!

"Listen to this," I say, "and sing along." I take my pipe and blow, very softly, a low note. It is the beginning of a song my papa used to sing to me, *"Cielito Lindo."*

"Hmmm, that sounds sweet as honey," Coyote says. "Let me try." He clears his throat and begins, "For when our hearts sing together, *ci-e-li-to lin-do,* love comes along . . ." His voice is soft and low.

"Bravo!" I shout.

"Bravo!" cry the owl, the bats, and the lizard.

The happy Coyote asks me where I am going. "I am on my way to Monterrey to become a glassblower."

"If you could teach me to sing, you can do anything!" he declares.

Then, as Coyote sings his sweet love song to *la luna,* Burro and I slip back into sleep.

Next morning, Burro and I start off with the sunrise, and at last we get to
Monterrey. There are many houses and buildings and everyone is in a hurry.
Before me is a factory where the furnace's giant mouth is full of bubbling glass.
    "Adiós, mi amigo," I say to Burro, and then step inside.

In front of me, four big men stand stiff as soldiers, puffing on long pipes. As their balloon cheeks shrink, glass bubbles appear and turn into tall bottles, medium bottles, and tiny bottles.

"What do you want?" their boss yells at me.

I cough and in a low voice I say, "*Por favor, señor . . .* I want to be a glassblower."

The men laugh. The boss winks and says, "Okay, *muchacho*. Let's see what you can do."

I twirl the end of my pipe in the hot glass just the way Papa does.

What is going to happen?

I close my eyes and gulp a deep breath. I puff out my cheeks and begin to play a song called *"Estrellita,"* about a little star.

When the men hear music, they laugh even harder. I think they will never stop, but then . . .

I remember how my pipe helped Burro, how it helped Roadrunner and Coyote. I blow, strong and steady, and when I open my eyes, I have made a star!

The men's mouths drop open in surprise.

I tap the star off into the sand to cool, and then I play *"Estrellita"* again. At the end of my pipe another glass star bursts out.